Nelson
GRAMMAR

PUPIL BOOK 4

WENDY WREN

Nelson

Book 4 – Contents

This symbol shows that you need to correct mistakes in the text.

Adjectives

Sometimes, a single **adjective** is not enough to describe a noun or pronoun.

We need to use a **phrase** (a group of words) to describe a thing so that the reader has a clear picture of what we are writing about.

We could describe the picture on the left by saying:

An old lady is crossing the road.

A reader would have a much clearer picture of the old lady if we wrote:

An old lady with a big floppy hat is crossing the road.

'Old' is a single adjective.

'With a big floppy hat' is an **adjective phrase**.

Joining two adjectives makes an adjective phrase.

A phrase is a group of words that does not contain a verb.

The garden, silent and deserted, was covered with snow.

The adjective phrase 'silent and deserted' describes the garden.

GRAMMAR *Focus*

Look for more than one adjective.

Copy the following sentences into your book.
Underline the **adjective phrase** in each sentence.

1 The weather, cold and wet, kept us in all day.

2 The handsome but sulky prince was in a bad mood.

3 The wood was dark and frightening in the moonlight.

4 Five small blue flowers had grown on the rubbish heap.

A Use these **adjective phrases** in sentences of your own.

1 sleek and graceful   2 with no shoes

3 frozen and slippery   4 with loud cries

5 old but useful

6 without an umbrella

B Write a sentence with an **adjective phrase** to describe each of these nouns.

1 meadow   2 feathers   3 cough

4 photograph   5 shepherd   6 dolphin

Remember, a phrase is a group of words that does not contain a verb.

Three of the examples below are **adjective phrases** and three are sentences.
Find the three adjective phrases.
Add a verb and any other words you need to make each one into a sentence.
Find the three sentences and write them with their correct punctuation.

1 thank you said Jim

2 Janet ran home

3 the poor injured duck

4 a shivering and frightened

5 give me that

6 with a heavy bag

Prefixes

'Pre' comes from the Latin word 'prae', meaning 'before'.

Letters added to the front of a word are called a **prefix**. Some prefixes can change a word so it means the opposite.

happy	**un**happy	wise	**un**wise
visible	**in**visible	sane	**in**sane
possible	**im**possible	patient	**im**patient
appear	**dis**appear	trust	**dis**trust
legal	**il**legal	legible	**il**legible
clockwise	**anti**clockwise	climax	**anti**climax

Prefixes have special meanings.
Here are some more common prefixes and their meanings.

Like 'pre', many prefixes come from Latin.

Prefix	Meaning	Examples	
bi	two	**bi**cycle	**bi**lingual
ex	out of	**ex**port	**ex**it
inter	between	**inter**val	**inter**national
mis	wrong	**mis**behave	**mis**judge
re	again	**re**place	**re**turn
sub	under	**sub**marine	**sub**way

GRAMMAR *Focus*

The opposite of a word is called its **antonym**.

A Use a **prefix** to make the opposite of each of these words. Write the words in your book and check them in a dictionary.

1	true	2	loyal	3	movable	4	secure
5	honour	6	pure	7	well	8	mobile
9	approve	10	logical	11	agree	12	active

B Copy the sentences below.
Add a **prefix** to one word in each sentence so that the sentence has the opposite meaning.

1 Did you obey the rules?

2 Will you lock the door?

3 What you want to do is possible.

Match each of the words in the box with its correct meaning.

| rewrite   incapable   invisible |
| disbelieve   recommence |

1 to begin again

2 to think that something is not true

3 not able to do something

4 not able to be seen

5 to put words on paper again

GRAMMAR *Extension*

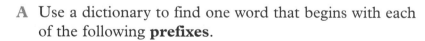

A Use a dictionary to find one word that begins with each of the following **prefixes**.

1 inter	2 bi	3 pro	4 pre
5 mono	6 sub	7 post	8 auto
9 al	10 re	11 ex	12 trans

B Put each word that you made in part A into a sentence of your own.

C Use a dictionary to help you to write the meaning of each of these words.

1 explosion	2 extension	3 invasion
4 preparation	5 biped	6 international
7 mistake	8 revise	9 submerge

Verbs

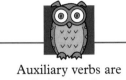

Auxiliary verbs are 'helper' verbs.

Sometimes we need more than one **verb** to make a sentence work properly.

We need to use an **auxiliary verb** to help the main verb. The verb 'to be' is often used as an auxiliary verb and tells us when something happens.

He **was** **teaching** me how to do this.
He **is** **teaching** me how to do this.
He **will** **teach** me how to do this.

Here are some more auxiliary verbs.

has	She **has** **gone** out.
have	I **have** **forgotten** my dinner money.
had	We **had** **seen** the fox many times.
must	You **must** **clean** the floor.
might	I **might** **catch** the early train.
could	I **could** **meet** you at twelve o'clock.
should	You **should** **wear** a helmet on your bike.
would	They **would** **enjoy** a picnic today.

GRAMMAR *Focus*

Copy the following sentences into your book.
Underline the **auxiliary verb** in each sentence.

1 She is feeling unwell today.

2 We would like to discuss the problem.

3 The telephone has rung seven times.

4 I must leave at six o'clock.

5 I could find the station on the map.

6 The photographs were taken last summer.

Copy the sentences below.
Use the **auxiliary verbs** *am, are, is, was* or *were* to fill the gaps.

1 Cowslips _____ growing in the meadow last year.

2 I _____ spreading butter on my bread before I put on the jam.

3 She _____ going abroad for her holidays.

4 We _____ hoping to finish this before we go.

5 He _____ playing tennis when he hurt his hand.

GRAMMAR *Extension*

A The sentences below are written in the present tense. Change the **two auxiliary verbs** in each sentence so that they are in the past tense.

1 I am thinking about what I am going to do.

2 We are walking to the town and then we are going to catch a bus.

3 They are wondering what they are going to find.

B The sentences below are written in the past tense. Change the **auxiliary verb** and the **main verb** so that each sentence is in the future tense.

1 I was meeting a friend after lunch.

2 We were hoping for sunny weather.

3 She was going outside for a few minutes.

Pronouns

A **pronoun** can be used instead of a noun.

The dog has a kennel.

It has a kennel.

Some pronouns show ownership or possession.
They are called **possessive pronouns**.

This coat is **mine**.

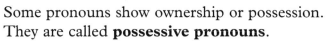

That coat is **yours**.

Here are some more possessive pronouns.

his	The book on the floor is **his**.
hers	This torn letter is **hers**.
mine	The red bicycle is **mine**.
ours	All the sheep in that field are **ours**.
theirs	Our garden is bigger than **theirs**.
yours	Is this **yours**?

GRAMMAR *Focus*

Copy the following sentences into your book.
Use **possessive pronouns** in place of the brown words.

1 Your writing is neater than my writing.

2 My pen is broken. Will you lend me your pen?

3 She has lost her pencil. Is this her pencil?

4 That's a blue pencil. It must be his pencil.

5 The teachers left some books here. I'm not sure which are their books.

Copy the sentences below.
Write a **possessive pronoun** in each gap.

1 "This chair is _____, and that chair is _____," said Ian to his sister.

2 "These games are _____," shouted the boys.

3 Carl made a model castle. Lynn helped him so it is _____ as well.

4 The children had to take some baby photographs to school. The twins were not sure if they could find _____.

5 The teacher asked for the homework. Katy and I hadn't brought _____.

GRAMMAR *Extension*

Write a sentence using each pair of **possessive pronouns**.

1 mine	yours
2 theirs	ours
3 his	hers
4 ours	his
5 hers	mine

Nouns

A suffix is an ending.

Nouns can be made from verbs, usually by adding a **suffix** like **ing**, **er** or **ment**.

verb	to paint	to manage
noun	the paint**ing**	the manag**er**
	the paint**er**	the manage**ment**

But be careful!
Sometimes the word changes slightly when a noun is made from a verb.

verb	to thieve
noun	the thief
	the theft

GRAMMAR *Focus*

Copy the following list of verbs into your book.
Next to each verb, write the matching **noun**.

Verb	Noun
to hate	exploration
to explain	loser
to laugh	runner
to explore	hatred
to lose	driver
to run	laughter
to drive	explanation

Check your answers in a dictionary. Some of the spellings are tricky.

Copy the sentences below.
Make a noun from the verb in brackets to fill the gap in each sentence.

1 Aziz made a good _____ . (to suggest)

2 We made an _____ about what to watch on television. (to agree)

3 The _____ to the cave was blocked by fallen rocks. (to enter)

4 The Big Book of _____ was very helpful for my project. (to know)

5 The old house needed many _____ . (to improve)

6 David had a slight _____ after the race. (to injure)

7 The _____ was sea-sick when the weather was rough. (to sail)

8 Stella was a very good _____ . (to swim)

Look up each of the following **nouns** in your dictionary. Write the meaning, and the verb from which it is made.

1	conversation	2	embarrassment
3	fertiliser	4	germination
5	hypnotism	6	imagination
7	judgement	8	lubrication
9	magnification	10	organisation

13

Nouns and verbs

Nouns and **verbs** can be singular or plural. When we use a **singular** noun we must use a **singular** verb.

The tunnel goes under the sea.

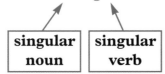

| singular noun | singular verb |

When we use a **plural** noun we must use a **plural** verb.

The cockerels crow every morning.

| plural noun | plural verb |

The words 'each' and 'every' always come before **singular** nouns.

Each flower has colourful petals.

Every petal is very delicate.

Collective nouns are always followed by **singular** verbs.

The herd lives on the hill.

The flock of birds circles overhead.

Sums of money and **popular food** are **singular**.

£2.50 is the price of that magazine.

Fish and chips is not a healthy meal.

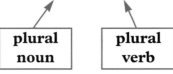

GRAMMAR *Focus*

Copy the following into your book.
Write whether each would be followed by a **singular** or a **plural verb**.

1 the sandals   2 the spoonful

3 each boy   4 eggs and bacon

5 this bunch   6 the pedals

7 every horse   8 80p

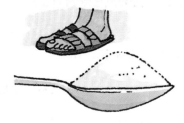

Copy the sentences below.
Choose the **singular** or the **plural verb** to complete each one.

1 Vandals wreck/wrecks other people's property.

2 We is/are careful about locking the door.

3 The group play/plays on Saturdays.

4 Sausage and mash is/are my favourite meal.

5 Each ticket has/have a number on it.

A Add a **predicate** to each of these subjects to make a sentence.

Remember, the predicate is all of the sentence except the subject.

1 One million pounds _____.

2 The orchestra _____.

3 Every tree _____.

4 Each new pupil _____.

5 Baked beans _____.

B Add a **subject** to each of these predicates to make a sentence.

The subject of a sentence is the person or thing written about.

1 _____ sparkles with jewels.

2 _____ gallop around the race course.

3 _____ was very long.

4 _____ were under the bed.

5 _____ are very late.

15

Adverbs

Sometimes, a single **adverb** is not enough to tell us how, when or where something happens.

We need to use two or three words to describe how, when or where something happens so that the reader has a clear picture of what we are writing about.

We could write about the picture on the left by saying:

The rocket took off **quickly**.

A reader would have a much clearer picture of what happened if we wrote:

The rocket took off **in a huge burst of flame**.

'In a huge burst of flame' is an **adverb phrase**, telling us **how** the rocket took off.

We could write:

The rocket took off **on Thursday night**.

'On Thursday night' is an **adverb phrase**, telling us **when** the rocket took off.

We could write:

The rocket took off **into the dark night sky**.

'Into the dark night sky' is an **adverb phrase**, telling us **where** the rocket took off.

A phrase is a group of words that does not contain a verb.

GRAMMAR *Focus*

Look for the words which tell you **how**, **when** or **where** the action takes place.

Copy the following sentences into your book. Underline the **adverb phrase** in each one.

1 The giant approached the village with loud, thudding footsteps.

2 Yesterday morning, I planted some seeds.

3 The painter climbed to the top of the ladder to paint the window frame.

4 We ran as quickly as we could.

5 The eagle built its nest on the mountain top.

A Use these **adverb phrases** in sentences of your own.

1 *from time to time*

2 *before sunrise*

3 *at the crossroads*

4 *in the middle of the field*

5 *carefully and slowly*

6 *with great confidence*

You can use any part of the verb. You do not have to use the verb family name.

B Write a sentence with an **adverb phrase** to describe how, when or where each of these verbs happened.

1 to mix	2 to measure	3 to depart
4 to discuss	5 to laugh	6 to cough

GRAMMAR *Extension*

A Three of the following are adverb phrases and three are sentences.
Copy the **adverb phrases** and add a verb and any other words you need to make them into sentences.

1 *before the first lesson*

2 *we'll meet at the corner*

3 *in front of the cinema*

4 *gasping for breath*

5 *simon rang the bell repeatedly*

6 *you must find that letter*

B Find the three sentences from part A.
Write them with their correct punctuation.

Check-up 1

Nouns

Write a **noun** that can be made from each verb.

1 to manage   2 to free   3 to paint
4 to laugh   5 to walk   6 to encourage

Adjectives

A Copy these sentences.
Underline the **adjective phrases**.

1 Antarctica is a cold and frozen land.
2 The bicycle with the punctured tyre is mine.
3 The birds pecked at the newly mown lawn.
4 The angry, wounded tiger ran into the jungle.

B Use these **adjective phrases** in sentences of your own.

1 brightly coloured   2 dirty and smelly
3 in the old coat   4 blue and still

Prefixes

Use a **prefix** to make the opposite of each word.

1 legal   2 accurate   3 perfect
4 respect   5 enjoyable   6 decided

Verbs

Copy these sentences.
Underline the **auxiliary verbs**.

1 I am drawing a flower and a tree.
2 The dolphin might jump out of the water.
3 The pollution of this river must stop.
4 We should plough the field tomorrow.
5 The lions have drunk at the water hole.

Pronouns

A Copy these sentences.
Underline the **possessive pronouns**.

1 This towel is mine.

2 That dog of theirs is very noisy.

3 I'm taking this book back to the library. Do you want me to take yours?

4 I like his painting better than hers.

B Use each of these **possessive pronouns** in a sentence of your own.

1 his   2 hers   3 mine

4 ours   5 theirs   6 yours

Nouns and verbs

A Use these words in sentences of your own.
Underline the **nouns** in red and the **verbs** in blue.

1 penguin   2 hospital   3 needles

4 students   5 is   6 have

7 croaks   8 were

B Use these **collective nouns** in sentences of your own.

1 queue   2 gang   3 forest

Adverbs

Copy these sentences and underline the **adverb phrases**.

1 The class listened in complete silence.

2 Tomorrow at midday the parade will begin.

3 From the top of the tree, I could see the old mill.

4 Dad was preparing a meal in the kitchen.

5 I could not get to sleep last night.

19

Sentences

Indirect speech is sometimes called **reported speech** because we report what somebody has said.

Direct speech is when we write the actual words that someone has spoken.

Inverted commas go around the spoken words.

Punctuation at the end of the spoken words goes before the inverted commas.

When a different person speaks we begin a new line.

"The driver got the bus stuck on the bridge today," said Meg.

"What happened?" asked Mum.

"The police came and sent for a tow truck. It took them ages to get it free. We were late for school!" replied Meg.

Indirect speech is when we write about what a person has said.

We don't use the actual spoken words so we don't need inverted commas.

Meg told her Mum that the bus had got stuck on the bridge. Mum wanted to know what happened and Meg said that the police and a tow truck came to free the bus but it took so long they were late for school.

GRAMMAR *Focus*

In your book, write which of these sentences use **direct speech** and which use **indirect speech**.

1 "Look at my swimming certificate," said Len.

2 Sonia said that she couldn't find the newspaper.

3 "Stop, thief!" shouted the policewoman as the burglar ran away.

4 Rob told his Dad that the computer was broken.

5 The doctor asked how long I had been feeling unwell.

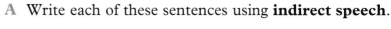

A Write each of these sentences using **indirect speech**.

1 "Would all passengers go to platform 8," boomed the voice over the loudspeaker.

2 "I like porridge for breakfast," said Dad.

3 "How long do I have to wait to be served?" snapped the customer.

4 "I've forgotten my lines!" groaned the actor.

B Write each of these sentences using **direct speech**.

1 Chris said that his book was very dull.

2 Owen wanted to know how far they still had to go.

3 The singer asked if many people had come to the show.

4 Martha encouraged Sandy to tell her what had happened.

A Write a conversation in **direct speech** between Malcolm and Emma about what they watched on television last night.
Remember to use inverted commas, punctuation and to begin a new line when a different person speaks.

B Write the same conversation between Malcolm and Emma in **indirect speech**.
Remember that you do not need inverted commas because you are not writing the words that were actually spoken.

Verbs

Remember! The subject is what the sentence is about.

When the subject of a sentence does the action, the verb is called an **active verb**.

The man **bought** a ticket.

'man' = subject of the sentence
'bought' = what the subject is doing

In this sentence, 'bought' is an active verb.

When the subject of the sentence has the action done to it, the verb is called a **passive verb**.

The ticket **was bought** by the man.

'ticket' = subject of the sentence
'was bought' = what was done to the subject

In this sentence, 'was bought' is a passive verb.

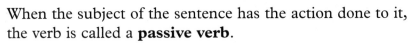

GRAMMAR *Focus*

Find the subject. Is the subject doing the action, or is the action being done to the subject?

Find the verb in each of these sentences.
In your book, write whether the verb is **active** or **passive**.

1   The judge banged on the table.

2   A sailor was hit by the rigging.

3   A few regular customers went into the shop every day.

4   The monster attacked the town.

5   One of the escalators was stopped by the shop manager.

6   The bridge fell into the river.

7   The library was broken into last night.

8   I have lost my dictionary.

Find the subject. Change the sentence so that the action is being done to the subject.

A Rewrite each of the following sentences, changing the verb from **active** to **passive**.
The first one has been done for you.

1 Our teacher read the class a story.
   A story was read to the class by the teacher.

2 The captain won a famous victory.

3 We heard thunder in the afternoon.

4 I tidied my room yesterday.

Find the subject. Change the sentence so that the subject is doing the action.

B Rewrite these sentences, changing the verb from **passive** to **active**.
The first one has been done for you.

1 The new vase was cracked by the boy.
   The boy cracked the new vase.

2 The windows were cleaned this morning by my Dad.

3 The play was disliked by the audience.

4 The house was shaded by the trees.

5 Rabbits are shot by some farmers.

GRAMMAR *Extension*

A Write sentences where each of these verbs are **active**.

1 to carry   2 to lift   3 to see

4 to write   5 to cover   6 to bury

B Rewrite the sentences from part A, making the verbs **passive**.

Suffixes

A **suffix** is a word ending.

The suffix **ed** tells us that an action has happened in the past.

> I smash**ed** the plate

The suffix **ing** is used with the verb 'to be' to tell us that an action is in the present tense or the past tense.

> I **am** throw**ing** the ball.
> I **was** throw**ing** the ball.

The suffix **er** makes a new word.

Lots of these new words are comparative adjectives, comparative adverbs or nouns.

> One lady was calm**er** than the other one.

When we add **ed**, **ing** or **er** to words, we sometimes have to double the last letter.

We usually double the last letter if the one before it is a single vowel.

ski**p**	ski**pped**	ski**pping**	ski**pper**
fit	fi**tted**	fi**tting**	fi**tter**

Comparative adverbs and comparative adjectives are used to compare things.

The vowels are **a, e, i, o** and **u.**

GRAMMAR *Focus*

Copy this table into your book and complete it.

Word	'ed' suffix	'ing' suffix	'er' suffix
warm	warmed	warming	warmer
jump	_____	_____	_____
fill	_____	_____	_____
wrap	_____	_____	_____
clean	_____	_____	_____
help	_____	_____	_____
count	_____	_____	_____

Remember, you may need to double the last letter.

Add the **suffix** ed, ing or er to complete each sentence.

1 This ice cream is big___ than that one.

2 The pirates were look___ for the treasure.

3 We search___ and search___ but we could not find it.

4 The run___ who was first received the medal.

5 Cook___ is one of my hobbies.

6 The long___ you take to get ready, the less time we will have for fish___ .

GRAMMAR *Extension*

Find the verb ending in 'ed'. Use the verb 'to be' and an 'ing' word in its place.

A Use the **suffix** ing to change these sentences into the present tense.

1 The birds circled overhead.

2 A stranger moved into the village.

3 The garage door creaked in the wind.

4 I tried hard with my fractions.

Find the two words that make up the present tense verb. Use one word with 'ed' instead.

B Use the **suffix** ed to change these sentences into the past tense.

1 We are wondering if our decision was the right one.

2 I am posting a letter to my friend.

3 They are electing the team captain.

4 We are sailing into the harbour.

Sentences

Clauses are small groups of words. They are similar to phrases, but clauses contain a proper verb.

The man was cold, so he wore his coat.

This sentence has two **verbs** and two **clauses**.

Clause 1 = The man was cold   **verb** = was
Clause 2 = so he wore his coat   **verb** = wore

In sentences with two clauses, one of the clauses is usually more important and is called the **main clause**.

The main clause in this sentence is 'The man was cold'. The main clause can usually be a sentence by itself.

The main clause does not have to come first.

After we had seen the elephants, we trudged back to our camp.

Main clause = we trudged back to our camp
Second clause = After we had seen the elephants

GRAMMAR *Focus*

Copy these sentences into your book.
Underline the **main clause** in each sentence.

The clause that is not the main clause usually begins with a conjunction, such as **and, but, so, although, when, because, after** or **before**.

1 We were ready to go when it started to rain.

2 The procession came down the main street and went into the park.

3 Although we played very well, we didn't win the match.

4 When I do my sums, I don't use a calculator.

5 If I make a mess in my room, I have to tidy up.

6 The volcano erupted and lava poured down its sides.

Write out the **two clauses** in each sentence and underline the **main clause**.

1 The famous violinist was nervous but she played very well.

2 I am curious to know where you are going and how you will get there.

3 If you park on a double yellow line, you will get a parking ticket.

4 The builder finished his work and put away his tools.

GRAMMAR *Extension*

A Add a **second clause** to each of these **main clauses**. You may be able to make more than one clause by using different conjunctions.

> Your second clause can begin with a conjunction.

1 The apple was rotten _____ .

2 I could see a town in the distance _____ .

3 My brother and I quarrelled _____ .

4 These feathers are similar_____ .

5 The radiator was leaking _____ .

B Add a **main clause** to each of these **second clauses**.

1 _____ and we enjoyed ourselves.

2 _____ when the race started.

3 Although I am a good swimmer _____ .

4 _____ because he was very generous.

5 Before the bridge was built _____ .

27

Adjectives

Possessive adjectives describe a noun, for example '**my** book'.
A **possessive pronoun** stands in place of a possessive adjective and a noun, for example, 'This book is **mine**.'

Its means 'belonging to it'.
It's means 'it is'.

Adjectives are sometimes called describing words because they tell us more about nouns.

an **unhappy** judge

a **neat** hedge

Possessive adjectives tell us who possesses (owns) a noun.

This is **his** badge

This is **her** sledge.

These are possessive adjectives:

my   your   his   her   our   its   their

GRAMMAR *Focus*

Copy the following sentences into your book.
Underline the **possessive adjectives**.

1 The computer in our classroom is not working properly.

2 If you can remember that far back your memory is very good.

3 The castle was well preserved but its tower was in ruins.

4 The champion beat his opponent easily.

5 Their quarrel lasted for days.

Copy the sentences below.
Fill each gap with a suitable **possessive adjective**.

1 I'll let you have _____ new address when we move.

2 The committee found it difficult to make _____ decision.

3 Katy was pleased because _____ friend was coming to stay for the weekend.

4 _____ tap was leaking so we called a plumber.

GRAMMAR *Extension*

A Write an ordinary **adjective** and a **possessive adjective** to describe each of these nouns.
The first one is done for you.

1 picture   *his colourful picture*

2 discussion   3 cough   4 breakfast

5 homework   6 table   7 birthday

B

We often mix up **its** and **it's**.
Its means 'belonging to'. **It's** means 'it is'.

Write *its* or *it's* in each gap to complete the sentences.

1 The dog slept in _____ kennel.

2 "_____ a ghost!" screamed Jenny.

3 _____ windier today than it was yesterday.

4 The kitten put out _____ sharp claws.

Adjectives

A clause has a verb, a phrase does not.

To make sentences more interesting, we can use **adjective phrases** and **adjective clauses**.

An adjective clause tells us more about a noun or pronoun in the main clause.

> We went to the shop **that sold camping equipment**.

Main clause = We went to the shop
Adjective clause = that sold camping equipment.

The adjective clause tells us more about the **shop** in the main clause.

Adjective clauses do the same job as adjectives and adjective phrases.
They all describe nouns and pronouns.

Adjective clauses begin with these words:

who   **which**   **that**

We use **who** when we are writing about a person.

> The nurse took care of the man **who had broken his arm**.

We use **which** or **that** when we are writing about an animal or a thing.

> Can you find the key **which fits this lock**?
> I saw the birds **that are nesting in our garage**.

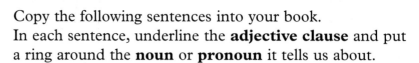

GRAMMAR *Focus*

Copy the following sentences into your book.
In each sentence, underline the **adjective clause** and put a ring around the **noun** or **pronoun** it tells us about.

1 I delivered the package which my mother had given to me.

2 Mark wrote to his friend who lives in Australia.

3 This is the badge which I bought at the zoo.

4 I want to find the boy who owns this bicycle.

Copy the sentences below.
Use *who* or *which* to fill each gap.

1 They travelled by bus _____ took a long time.

2 I have thrown away the chair _____ had a broken arm.

3 Will you find someone _____ can take care of the dog?

4 There were several passengers _____ had lost their tickets.

5 Find the pencil _____ has a rubber on the end.

GRAMMAR *Extension*

A Add **adjective clauses** to these main clauses to complete the sentences.

1 I baked the bread _____.

2 The police went to the house _____.

3 They looked for the girl _____.

4 We visited the old lady _____.

> Remember! Your adjective clause needs a proper verb.

B Add main clauses to the following **adjective clauses** to complete the sentences.

1 _____ who likes to play football.

2 _____ which grows in our garden.

3 _____ that I like best.

4 _____ which fell on our house.

> Remember! Your main clause needs a proper verb. A main clause can be a sentence by itself.

Verbs

An auxiliary verb is a 'helper' verb.

Sometimes we need more than one **verb** to make a sentence work properly.

We need to use an **auxiliary verb** to help the main verb.

The verb families '**to be**' and '**to have**' are often used as auxiliary verbs.

> The wreckage **is floating** in the harbour.
>
> The candle **has burnt** very low.

The words **can** and **may** are used as auxiliary verbs but they have special meanings.

Can means 'is able to'.
May means 'has permission to'.

> He **can** answer that question.
> You **may** leave the room.

Shall and **will** are often used as auxiliary verbs.

Shall comes after **I** and **we**.
Will comes after **you**, **they**, **he**, **she** and **it**.

> **I shall** go out.
> **They will** go out.

Shall and will are part of the verb family '**to be**'.

If we want to write a strong statement, we use them the other way around.

> **I will** go out!
> **You shall** go out!

GRAMMAR *Focus*

Copy the following sentences into your book.
Underline the **auxiliary verbs**.

1. The picture was hanging on that wall.
2. I have forgotten to do my homework.
3. I can jump over the fence.
4. We may buy some sweets.
5. The shield will keep you safe.

A Copy the sentences below.
Use the **auxiliary verbs** *can* or *may* to fill each gap.

1 This book is quite difficult but I am sure you ____ read it.

2 You ____ go out to play when you have changed your clothes.

3 You ____ get to the top of that tree with a ladder.

4 You ____ not cross the road by yourself.

B Copy the sentences below.
Use the **auxiliary verbs** *shall* or *will* to fill each gap.

1 I ____ write very neatly today.

2 "You ____ eat all the carrots!" said Mum.

3 He ____ find these sums very difficult.

4 "We ____ not go to bed!" shouted the twins.

GRAMMAR *Extension*

Write sentences of your own using the following pairs of verbs.
Underline the **auxiliary verb** in each sentence.

1 has received   2 will recognise

3 can finish   4 may drop

5 is dodging   6 was carrying

7 shall obey   8 will do

9 may begin   10 can find

Adverbs

Adverb clauses do the same job as adverbs and adverb phrases. They give us more information about verbs.

To make sentences more interesting, we can use **adverb phrases** and **adverb clauses**.

An **adverb clause** tells us more about the verb in the main clause.

Adverb clauses begin with conjunctions.

The train has stopped **because the engine broke down**.

The adverb clause 'because the engine broke down' tells us why the train **has stopped**.

The train will start again **when they fix the engine**.

The adverb clause 'when they fix the engine' tells us when the train **will start** again.

The train will start again **if they fix the engine**.

The adverb clause 'if they fix the engine' tells us what must happen so the train **can start** again.

The train has started again **although no one has fixed the engine**.

The adverb clause 'although no one has fixed the engine' tells us that nothing has been done but the train has **still started**.

Adverb clauses can also begin with 'even though' and 'even if'.

GRAMMAR *Focus*

Copy the following sentences into your book.
In each sentence, underline the **adverb clause** and put a ring around the verb it tells us about.

1 The prisoner escaped because the guard was asleep.

2 I will do my homework when I have had something to eat.

3 I can't polish my shoes if there is no polish.

because	if
unless	although
even if	
even though	

Copy the sentences below.
Choose words from the box to complete these **adverb clauses**.

1 We will go to the village shop _____ we have time.

2 You cannot ride your bike _____ you wear your helmet.

3 The doctor works very late _____ there are lots of people waiting to see her.

4 I have to find my bag _____ I am late for school.

GRAMMAR *Extension*

Adverb clauses, like adjective clauses, can come at the beginning of a sentence.

A Add **adverb clauses** to these main clauses to complete the sentences.

1 The garage was broken into _____ .

2 _____ you will get wet.

3 You must obey the rules _____ .

4 _____ we don't have to go.

B Add main clauses to these **adverb clauses** to complete the sentences.

1 _____ because the scissors are blunt.

2 Although I am disappointed _____ .

3 _____ even though I think I am right.

4 If the shepherd leaves the sheep _____ .

Adjectives

> Adjectives are describing words.
>
> We use them to make our writing more interesting and to give the reader a clear picture of what we are writing about.

Some **adjectives** are formed from verbs:

Verb	Adjective	Example
to bend	bent	a **bent** pin
to burn	burnt	the **burnt** toast
to groan	groaning	the **groaning man**

Some verbs are used as **adjectives**:

Verb	Use as an adjective
to rock	**rocking** chair
to skate	**skating** rink
to build	**building** block

Some **adjectives** are formed from nouns:

Noun	Adjective	Example
skill	skilful	a **skilful** player
child	childish	a **childish** joke
danger	dangerous	a **dangerous** situation

Some nouns are used as **adjectives**:

Noun	Use as an adjective
book	**book** cover
window	**window** sill
town	**town** hall

GRAMMAR *Focus*

Copy the following sentences into your book. Underline the **adjective** in each sentence and write whether it is formed from a **verb** or a **noun**.

1 The crying baby was in her pram.

2 The wooden hut was never used.

3 The dried flowers were thrown away.

4 The warlike warriors attacked at dawn.

to run	to weave
to read	to swim
to terrify	to break

A Use the **verbs** in the box to make **adjectives** to complete these sentences.

1 The _____ rug was made on a loom.

2 I practised diving into the _____ pool.

3 Four times around the _____ track is eight hundred metres.

4 The _____ storm woke me up.

5 I have finished my _____ book.

6 I can't hold a fork with my _____ arm.

rectangle	music
dread	stone
generosity	dirt

B Use the **nouns** in the box to make **adjectives** to complete the sentences.

1 How many _____ instruments can you play?

2 The _____ path hurt my feet.

3 The box is a _____ shape.

4 Thank you for your _____ donation.

5 What a _____ mistake to make.

6 The _____ boy needed a wash.

Use the following **nouns** as **adjectives** in sentences of your own.

1 village	2 fire	3 cricket
4 water	5 tennis	6 paper

Check-up 2

Sentences

A Write each of these sentences using **direct speech**.

1 David said that he had been on holiday.

2 Shehzad asked what the time was.

3 The policeman wanted to know who owned the canal boat.

B Write each of these sentences using **indirect speech**.

1 "Where are we going?" asked Mike.

2 "There are too many people on this bus!" shouted the driver.

3 "It's too early to go to bed," moaned Sally.

C Copy these sentences.
Underline the **main clause** in each.

1 It's necessary to water the plants although it has rained today.

2 Before the sun sets, we must find our way out of this wood.

3 A dictionary is very useful because it tells you the meaning of words.

D Join each pair of sentences, using *who* or *which* to make a **main clause** and an **adjective clause**.

1 I needed a new bag. I could take it to school.

2 We have two mice. They are white.

3 I visited a friend. He lives by the sea.

Adverbs

Add an **adverb clause** to each of these **main clauses**.

1 *The gold ring slipped off my finger _____ .*

2 *The secretary typed my letter _____ .*

3 *_____ we discovered an old house.*

Suffixes

Add the **suffixes** *ed*, *ing* or *er* to complete these sentences.

1 *The clean__ swept the floor and polish__ the windows.*

2 *The teach__ was look__ for some chalk.*

3 *I have climb__ a high__ mountain than you have.*

Verbs

A Find the **verb** in each of the sentences below. Write whether the verb is **active** or **passive**.

  1 The explosion was heard for miles around.

  2 The buses crawled slowly along the road.

  3 The packet was delivered by the courier.

B In the following sentences, fill each gap with *can* or *may*.

1 *The children _____ have a dog if they look after it.*

2 *I _____ meet you at one o'clock.*

3 *You _____ write more neatly than that.*

Adjectives

A Write the **adjectives** that are formed from the following nouns and verbs.

  1 to fall   2 fright   3 to fry   4 rock

B Use these **possessive adjectives** in sentences of your own.

  1 my   2 her   3 its   4 your

Suffixes

Adding a suffix often changes the spelling of a word. Always check in a dictionary.

A **suffix** is a word ending.

A suffix added to a verb family name changes the **tense**.

family name	suffix 'ed'	suffix 'ing'
to talk	talk**ed**	talk**ing**
to row	row**ed**	row**ing**
to wink	wink**ed**	wink**ing**

Adding a suffix to a word can also change the job that the word does in a sentence.

use = verb   use**ful** = adjective

pain = noun   pain**ful** = adjective

operate = verb   oper**ation** = noun

imagine = verb   imagin**ation** = noun

happy = adjective   happi**ness** = abstract noun

weak = adjective   weak**ness** = abstract noun

Here are some more common suffixes:

amuse**ment**   manage**able**   tire**less**   serv**ant**

GRAMMAR *Focus*

Check your spelling in a dictionary!

Copy the following sentences into your book.

Use the **suffixes** *ful*, *tion* or *ness* to complete them.

The words in brackets are clues.

1 Which _____ do we take? (direct)

2 _____ falls quickly near the Equator. (dark)

3 You need to be very _____ if you climb on these rocks. (care)

4 These _____ sums are very difficult. (subtract)

5 He is very keen on sport and _____ . (fit)

6 The view from the top of the mountains was _____ . (wonder)

A Add **suffixes** to these words to change them into **adjectives**.

1 beauty	2 care	3 hope
4 enjoy	5 punish	6 believe

B Add **suffixes** to these words to change them into **abstract nouns**.

1 weak	2 kind	3 gentle
4 encourage	5 satisfy	6 situate

GRAMMAR *Extension*

Here are some more common **suffixes**:

bullock	vigorous	invasion
nursery	victorious	different

A Write sentences, using the words from the box above.

B Find a word with a **suffix** to match each of these definitions.

1 a baby duck
2 very well known
3 willing to help
4 likely to cause injury or death
5 someone's job
6 the opposite of daylight
7 giving money for goods or services

Sentences

All **sentences** begin with a capital letter.

All sentences end with:

a full stop	The dog was asleep.
a question mark	What time is it?
or an exclamation mark	The house is burning!

Commas are often used to help us understand the sense of a sentence.

We use commas between items in a list, or between groups of words.

> My teacher told me to learn to spell alphabet, elephant, prophet and pheasant.

We use **and** or **or** between the last two items in a list, instead of a comma.

We use commas to separate the actual words spoken in direct speech from the rest of the sentence.

> "I came early to get a good seat," said Fiona.

We use commas between parts of a sentence to tell the reader where to make a short pause.

> The hospital, which was built in the nineteenth century, will be closing down.
>
> "No, I won't answer the telephone," said Leah.
>
> "That's a good photograph, isn't it?" cried Steve.

GRAMMAR *Focus*

Copy the following sentences into your book.
Add **commas** where they are needed.

1. I did maths English PE and music today.

2. Peter lost his pen his ruler his rubber and his pencil sharpener.

3. Thought bought sought nought and fought are rhyming words.

4. I have invited Ruth Eamon Shah and John.

A The punctuation has been missed out after the spoken words in these direct speech sentences.
Copy each sentence and add a **comma**, a **question mark** or an **exclamation mark**.

1 "The entrance is blocked" explained Tom.

2 "I'm going to be really late" cried Ben.

3 "Is it bedtime" asked Lena.

B Add commas to these sentences to show the reader where to make a short pause.

1 "Yes I would like to go to the cinema."

2 "He hurt his arm falling off his bike didn't he?"

3 "You will find that book won't you?"

GRAMMAR *Extension*

Commas often go around phrases and clauses in sentences.
The phrases and clauses give us extra information. If they were left out, the sentence would still make sense.

> The clown, running around the ring, made everyone laugh.
> The clown made everyone laugh.

Put **commas** around the phrases and clauses in the following sentences.

1 The customer angry and impatient shouted at the shop assistant.

2 My sister who is four years younger than me starts school next week.

Pronouns

A **pronoun** takes the place of a noun.

> The driver parked the delivery van outside the shop.
> **He** parked the delivery van outside the shop.

The following pronouns are called **relative pronouns**:

> who   whom   whose   which   that

Relative pronouns are special because they do two jobs.
1 They take the place of nouns.
2 They act as **conjunctions**, and they are **related** to the noun that comes before them in a sentence.

> The passenger caught the train.
> The train was going to Cardiff.

> The passenger caught the train **which** was going to Cardiff.

'Who' is always used for people.
'Which' and 'that' are used for animals and things.

Conjunctions are joining words.

GRAMMAR *Focus*

Copy the following sentences into your book. Use the **relative pronouns** *who* or *which* to fill the gaps.

1 That's the badger _____ comes into our garden.

2 This letter is from my pen friend _____ lives in America.

3 I want to go to the park _____ has a boating lake.

4 The doctor _____ visited me was very kind.

5 The topic _____ we are doing in school is very interesting.

Join each pair of sentence using *who, which* or *that*.

1 I found an old coin. The coin was used in Roman times.

2 We have two cousins. Our cousins live by the sea.

3 Sam bought a book. The book was about fishing.

GRAMMAR *Extension*

'Whom' and 'whose' are **relative pronouns** but they are used in a special way.

'Whom' is used for people as the **object** of a verb.

I ← saw → the old lady. →

| **subject** | **verb** | | **object** |

This is **the old lady** whom I saw.

| **object** | **relative pronoun** | **subject** | **verb** |

'Whose' is used to replace a **possessive adjective**.

This is the old lady. **Her** cat is called Gibbs.

| **possessive adjective** |

This is the old lady **whose** cat is called Gibbs.

| **relative pronoun** |

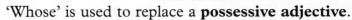

Use *whom* or *whose* to fill the gaps in these sentences.

1 I know the man _____ car was stolen.

2 From _____ did you borrow this book?

3 _____ bag is this?

Sentences

Sentences contain **clauses**.
A **main clause** is a sentence in itself.

The girl washed her face.

It has a **subject** – 'the girl'.
It has a **predicate** – 'washed her face'.
It has a **proper verb** in the predicate – 'washed'.

An **adjective clause** tells us more about the **noun** in the main clause and has a proper verb.

I want to see the man who won the race.

The main clause is 'I want to see the man'.
The adjective clause is 'who won the race'.

An **adverb clause** tells us more about the **verb** in the main clause.

The man won the race because he ran so quickly.

The main clause is 'The man won the race'.
The adverb clause is 'because he ran so quickly'.

Adjective clauses begin with **who**, **which** or **that**.

Adverb clauses begin with a conjunction.

GRAMMAR *Focus*

Copy the following sentences into your book.
Underline the **main clauses**.

1 The creature slipped into the pool and swam away.

2 Before you go out you must have something to eat.

3 After the match the winners were presented with the cup.

4 I will practise my signature on that piece of paper.

5 I hit the ball and broke the window.

Copy the sentences below.
Underline the **adjective clauses** in red and the **adverb clauses** in blue.

1 Although it is a warm day, you must take your coats.

2 I will wash the bicycle which is muddy.

3 The trip was cancelled because of the rain.

4 We will invite the twins who live on the farm.

GRAMMAR *Extension*

Remember!
Adjective clauses begin with who, which, that.

Adverb clauses begin with conjunctions.

A Complete these sentences by adding **adjective clauses** of your own.

1 This is the kitten _____.

2 Have you seen the rocket _____ ?

3 We saw the rider _____.

4 Can I speak to the teacher _____ ?

B Complete these sentences by adding **adverb clauses** of your own.

1 The little boy was naughty _____.

2 _____ will you let me know?

3 The zebra walked to the waterhole _____.

4 _____ you cannot watch that television programme.

Verbs

When we use **verbs** to tell us about something that has happened in the past, we use the **past tense**.

To make the past tense, we usually add **d** or **ed** to the verb family name.

The kittens play**ed**. The man signall**ed**.

When we want to write the past tense to show an action has gone on for some time or something else happens at the same time, we use a verb ending in **ing** with an **auxiliary verb**.

The children **were swimming** when it began to rain.

Auxiliary verbs are 'helper' verbs.

We can make the past tense in another way.
If two actions have happened in the past but one is 'further back' than the other one, we use 'had' and a past tense verb ending in **ed**.

I **had reached** the station before the train left.
The chef **had roasted** the chicken and then cooked the peas.
We found the shop but it **had closed**.

Some verbs do not make their past tense with **ed**. For example, write – wrote, keep – kept.

GRAMMAR *Focus*

Copy the following sentences into your book.
Underline the **past tense verbs** in each sentence.

Remember! Past tense verbs often have more than one word.

1 We were looking for our cat all day.

2 The comedian laughed and joked with the audience.

3 They had lived in a cottage before they moved to a new house.

Complete this table, using the three ways you know of making the **past tense**.

Verb family name	past tense	past tense – 'to be' and 'ing'	past tense – 'had'
to talk	I talked	I was talking	I had talked
to find	we found	we were finding	we had found
to see	they ____	____ ____ ____	____ ____ ____
to jump	you ____	____ ____ ____	____ ____ ____
to sleep	we ____	____ ____ ____	____ ____ ____
to throw	he ____	____ ____ ____	____ ____ ____
to sing	she ____	____ ____ ____	____ ____ ____

GRAMMAR *Extension*

Write a sentence in the **past tense** that includes each pair of actions below.
Action 1 happens first, before action 2.
The first one is done for you.

	Action 1	**Action 2**
1	watch a film	go to bed

I had watched a film before I went to bed.

2	walk	storm blows up
3	do homework	play tennis
4	eat breakfast	post arrives
5	write a story	go home

Sentences

A sentence can end with a question mark or an exclamation mark, as well as a full stop.

Direct speech is when we write the actual words that someone has spoken.

"Did you see the explosion?" asked Greg.
Greg asked, "Did you see the explosion?"

Sometimes we split the spoken words, so we have to be very careful with the punctuation.

"I saw the building was on fire," said Greg, "and I saw the explosion."

The sentence has been split by the words 'said Greg', so we use two sets of inverted commas and put a **comma** after 'said Greg'.

"I saw the building was on fire," said Greg. "I rushed over and heard the explosion."

This time, Greg said two sentences.
We still use two sets of inverted commas but we put a full stop after 'said Greg', before we begin the next sentence.

GRAMMAR *Focus*

Copy the following sentences into your book.
Underline the **spoken words**.

1 "I won this medal," said Lesley, "for coming first in the high jump."

2 "Where did you find that fossil?" asked Pam.

3 "You can ring me at work," explained Nick, "if you need to get in touch with me."

4 The climber shouted, "Get away from the edge!"

5 "I'm not very musical," mumbled Grace. "I prefer art."

Copy these sentences and put in the missing **punctuation** and **capital letters**.

1 that was a good goal shouted Sandy but we've got to score another one

2 go to the shop and buy some bread said Helen the money is in my purse

3 this photograph was taken last year said Rory we were on holiday at the seaside

4 we must be very quiet whispered Monica or we will wake the baby

5 i'm very tired moaned Chris i stayed up too late last night

6 can you find my blue shoes asked Mum and give them a polish

The words in the box can all be used instead of 'said'.

cried   yelled   muttered   laughed
sobbed   shrieked   boasted

Use each one in a **direct speech sentence** of your own.
Try to use some of them in between the spoken words.

51

Sentences

A **simple sentence** is made up of one main clause.

The hawk soared in the air.

A **compound sentence** is made up of two or more simple sentences joined by 'and', 'but' or 'or'.

The hawk soared in the air.	simple sentence
We watched it disappear in the distance.	simple sentence
The hawk soared in the air **and** we watched it disappear in the distance.	compound sentence
We were caught in a traffic jam.	simple sentence
We made it on time.	simple sentence
We were caught in a traffic jam **but** we made it on time.	compound sentence
It might rain tomorrow.	simple sentence
It might be fine.	simple sentence
It might rain tomorrow **or** it might be fine.	compound sentence

GRAMMAR *Focus*

Compound sentences have two main clauses. Each main clause is a sentence on its own.

Make **compound sentences** from these pairs of simple sentences. Write them in your book.

1 My sandal is broken. I think I can mend it.

2 The library was busy. There was nowhere to sit.

3 I might have pizza for lunch. I might have soup.

4 I like this poem. I don't like that one.

5 The bird's feathers were blue. Its beak was hooked.

Copy these **compound sentences**.
Underline the two **main clauses** in each sentence and put a ring around the **conjunction**.

> The conjunction is part of the second clause.

1 The famous explorer went to Africa and she stayed there for many years.

2 The volcano erupted and lava poured down its sides.

3 I enjoy playing basketball but I'm too tired to play now.

4 Are you going shopping on Friday or will you wait until Saturday morning?

5 It's my birthday today and I am going to have a party.

GRAMMAR *Extension*

Add a **conjunction** and a **main clause** to make each of these simple sentences into a **compound sentence**.

> The conjunctions you can use to make compound sentences are **and**, **but** or **or**.

1 The diver was looking for pearls _____ .

2 My head is aching _____ .

3 The factory is closing down _____ .

4 I might go for a swim _____ .

5 I may have misjudged you _____ .

Sentences

A **simple sentence** is made up of one main clause.

> The election was held on Thursday.

A **compound sentence** is made up of two or more simple sentences joined by 'and', 'but' or 'or'.

> The election was held on Thursday **and** the result was announced on Friday.

A **complex sentence** is made up of two or more clauses which are not of equal importance.
There is one **main clause** in a complex sentence.
Other clauses are joined to it by these words:

The conjunctions **and**, **but** and **or** are used in compound sentences not in complex sentences.

Conjunctions			Pronouns
before	where	unless	who
until	because	so	which
although	while	as	when
wherever	even though	after	whose
if			

main clause → **The house had been empty for many years** before we bought it.

The clause 'before we bought it' is not a sentence on its own. It needs the main clause to make sense.

GRAMMAR *Focus*

Copy these **complex sentences** into your book.
Underline the **main clause** in each sentence.

1 The guitar was broken before I borrowed it.

2 We climbed the mountain although it was very steep.

3 My sister will come over when she has finished work.

4 The people next door have a noisy dog which barks all day.

Join these pairs of simple sentences to make **complex sentences**.

Remember! Don't use **and**, **but** or **or**.

1 The microscope isn't working. I checked it this morning.

2 We are going on holiday. We have bought some new suitcases.

3 The flowers died. I watered them every day.

4 We saw the wrecked ship. It had crashed on the rocks.

GRAMMAR *Extension*

A Complete these as **compound sentences**.

1 The magician pulled a rabbit out of a hat _____.

2 The sheep were grazing in the field _____

_____.

3 We grow rhubarb in the garden _____.

4 She put scissors on the table _____.

B Complete these as **complex sentences**.

1 He was very frightened _____.

2 I can't go to school _____.

3 The children had to play inside_____.

4 I enjoyed the mystery story _____.

5 We were almost asleep _____.

Sentences

We need to look very carefully at what we write to see if we can improve it.

We can improve our writing by **changing some of the words**.

> I **got** a **nice** present for my birthday.

'Got' and 'nice' are words that are often used but there are better words.

> I **received** a **wonderful** present for my birthday.

We can improve our writing by expanding it.
Adding **words**, **phrases** and **clauses** to make it more interesting.

> The elephant drank the water.

> The **large, grey** elephant **stretched out its long, flexible trunk to take a drink of refreshing** water **from the cool, shaded pool.**

Look at each sentence you write and ask yourself whether you could add more details to answer these questions:

What kind? How many? How much?	adjectives, adjective phrases, adjective clauses

When? How? Where? How often?	adverbs, adverb phrases, adverb clauses

GRAMMAR *Focus*

In your book, rewrite these sentences to **improve** them. Replace the green words with more interesting words.

1 Our *nice* hedge had grown *a bit* this spring.

2 "I've *got a lot* of work to do," said Harry.

3 I *like* cold weather because I've *got* a really warm coat.

4 "I *like* this topic *a lot*," said Nancy.

Rewrite these sentences to give details which answer the questions in brackets.

1 The trees are growing. (What kind? Where?)

2 The children played football. (What kind? Where? How?)

3 The jockey won the race. (What kind? When? How?)

4 Can you see the butterfly? (What kind? Where?)

5 I walked into the valley. (How? What kind? Where?)

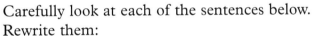

GRAMMAR *Extension*

Carefully look at each of the sentences below.
Rewrite them:

A to include more **interesting words** than got, said, like, bit, nice, lot, big and little;

B to include words, phrases and clauses which give the reader **more detail**.

1 A little bird sat on the tree.

2 The bus got stuck.

3 "I've lost my ticket," said Linda.

4 Would you like an ice cream?

5 The wind was a bit strong.

6 I got a nice jacket.

7 You can get a lot in this bucket.

8 "Did you have a nice time?" said Dad.

9 "Did you see the big bull?" said Katy.

10 That meal was nice.

Sentences

Moving in from the left-hand margin is called 'indenting'.

A **paragraph** is a group of sentences about one main idea.

Dividing a long piece of writing into paragraphs makes it easier for the reader to follow.

We sometimes set out the paragraph so that the first line begins about 20 mm in from the left-hand margin.

Early morning on the farm was always a busy time. Cows to be milked, chickens to feed and a hundred and one other jobs to be done.

Anna climbed out of bed as soon as her alarm went off. She washed and dressed quickly as she had many things to do before breakfast.

When she arrived in the kitchen her mother was already busy, baking bread and getting things ready for the first meal of the day. Anna set the table and then went outside.

After an hour of hard work, Anna had only the chickens to feed before she could eat herself. She scattered the corn about the yard, washed her hands under the outside tap and went inside.

Each paragraph is about one main idea:

Paragraph 1: Introducing the reader to the farm
Paragraph 2: Introducing the reader to Anna
Paragraph 3: Moving the scene from Anna's bedroom to the kitchen
Paragraph 4: Moving the story on in time.

GRAMMAR *Focus*

Use interesting words and give as much detail as possible.

Write the **first three paragraphs** of a story called 'The Dark Cave'.

Paragraph 1: Give a detailed description of the cave.
Paragraph 2: Introduce two characters who are exploring the cave.
Paragraph 3: Explain what happens to the two characters in the cave.

Read these **paragraphs** about animal environments and answer the questions.

Animals live in many different environments, such as hot, dry deserts, cold forbidding polar regions and high mountains.

In the desert, temperatures can reach over 50° C (120° F) during the day. There is not much water and animals have to keep cool without losing too much water by evaporation. They can shelter underground or in scarce shady areas. Animals that do spend time in the sun move in a special way so that as little of their bodies as possible touch the hot sand.

In the polar regions, the temperature can fall as low as –80° C (–112° F) in the winter. Here, animals have to keep warm and one way to do this is to stay under the snow in dens.

Living in the mountains, animals often experience low temperatures and harsh winds. They survive by sheltering in caves or on rock ledges, coming out during the day to look for food.

1   How many paragraphs has the writer used?

2   For each paragraph, write a sentence to explain the main idea.

A   Find a short story you have enjoyed reading. Answer the following questions about the **first four paragraphs**.

1   What is the main idea in each paragraph?

2   Explain why the first paragraph is, or is not, a good opening to the story.

B   Choose one of the following titles and write **one paragraph** of five to ten sentences about the topic. Underline one sentence in your paragraph to show what is the main idea.

A really bad day
Looking after a pet
My favourite sport

Check-up 3

Adjectives

A Copy these sentences and underline the **adjective phrase** in each.

1 Eight large, hissing geese crossed the road.
2 The sea, calm and blue, sparkled in the sunlight.
3 The elephant with the longest tusks is the oldest.

B Copy the following sentences.
Fill each gap with a suitable **possessive adjective**.

1 _____ boots were dirty so we had to clean them.
2 Sam and _____ friend went camping.
3 They packed _____ bags before breakfast.

C Add an **adjective clause** to complete each sentence.

1 This is the spaceship _____.
2 The children went to the park _____.
3 We saw the shopkeeper _____.

D Make **adjectives** from these nouns and verbs.

1 to colour   2 grass   3 to frighten
4 to scream   5 bravery   6 envy

Prefixes

Add a **prefix** to each word to make its opposite.

1 like   2 controllable   3 capable
4 literate   5 passable   6 climax

Verbs

A Copy the sentences below.
Underline the **auxiliary verb** in each sentence.

1 We must find our key.

2 I would hate to swim in that dirty river.

3 If you go early, you might get a good seat.

B Copy these sentences.
Use the **auxiliary verbs** can or may to fill each gap.

1 We ____ see the windmill from here.

2 You ____ have more potatoes when you finish those.

3 If you ____ tidy the bookcase I will be very pleased.

C Copy these sentences.
Choose the **singular** or **plural verb** to complete each one.

1 The penguins was/were diving for fish.

2 The herd of cows need/needs to be milked.

3 £3 is/are the price of the tickets.

D Rewrite these sentences, changing the verb from **passive** to **active**.

1 The tree was blown down by the wind.
2 The topmost leaves were eaten by the giraffes.
3 The window was broken by a stone.

E Copy these sentences.
Underline the **past tense verbs** in each one.

1 Our newspaper was delivered late today.

2 The gardener had cut the hedge before the birds built their nests.

3 I completed the quiz in ten minutes.

Pronouns

A Use **possessive pronouns** to replace the blue words.

1 May I ride your bicycle? My bicycle has a puncture.

2 Their car is newer than our car.

3 You know that pen you found? Sally says it's her pen.

B Join each pair of sentences using a **relative pronoun**.

1 Fred watched a programme. It was about whales.

2 I have an uncle. He is a policeman.

3 Have you seen the kittens? They were born on the farm.

Nouns

Write a **noun** that is formed from each of these verbs.

1 to write	2 to imagine	3 to grow
4 to play	5 to injure	6 to live

Adverbs

A Copy these sentences.
Underline the **adverb phrases**.

1 Two days ago I visited my aunt.

2 The boy kicked the ball hard and straight.

3 The fox made its den in the middle of the wood.

B Write an **adverb clause** to complete each sentence.

1 The match was cancelled _____ .

2 _____ you will get a sore throat .

3 I will go swimming again _____ .

Suffixes

A Change these verb family names into the **present tense** using the **suffix** 'ing'.

1 to write 2 to live 3 to stop 4 to receive

B Change these verb family names into the **past tense** using the **suffix** 'ed'.

1 to paint 2 to dodge 3 to thread 4 to close

C Add a **suffix** to each of these words to change it into an **adjective**.

1 fever 2 saint 3 dust 4 danger

D Add a **suffix** to each of these words to change it into an **abstract noun**.

1 weary 2 dark 3 serve 4 weak

Sentences

A Change these direct speech sentences into **indirect speech**.

1 "I am enjoying myself," said Len.

2 "This soup is cold!" complained Robert.

3 "Have you read the newspaper?" I asked Dad.

B Add capital letters and punctuation to these **direct speech** sentences.

1 can you get the bread said Helen and some butter

2 why does it always rain moaned Chris when I want to go out

3 one of the cedar trees fell down cried John and hit the car

C Copy these sentences and underline the **main clauses**.

1 I have to hurry because I am already late.

2 Although it snowed, I wasn't cold.

3 Brush your teeth before you go to bed.

D Copy these sentences.
Add **commas** where they are needed.

1 I would like some carrots turnips potatoes beans and sprouts.

2 He's wearing my sweater isn't he?

3 The gate unpainted and broken creaked in the wind.

E Join each pair of simple sentences to make a **compound sentence**.

1 I need to go to the doctor. I don't have time.

2 I'm sure I heard the phone. Was it the front doorbell?

3 The car's tyre was punctured. The bumper was bent.

F Complete these as **compound sentences**.

1 I wrote a long letter _____.

2 She plays volleyball _____.

3 We had a noisy celebration _____.

G Improve these sentences by using more **interesting** words and more **detail**.

1 I got a bad mark in the test.

2 We had a nice day and did quite a lot.

3 "The cat got stuck up the tree," said Mandy.

H Write two **paragraphs** on one of the following subjects. Underline the sentence in each paragraph which contains the main idea.

A School Trip   Sports Day   A Lucky Escape